Contract-to-Close:
A Step-by-Step Manual for Buyer Agents

Kevin Reid Shirley

Contract-to-Close: A Step-by-Step Manual for Buyer Agents

Copyright 2017 Kevin Reid Shirley

Table of Contents

Introduction

Real estate isn't rocket science, at least on the surface: Put buyers and sellers together, help guide them through the negotiation and on to a successful settlement, collect a commission check, exit stage left, repeat. Alas, the devil though — as they say — is in the details. And details there are. Many of them. It seems that each year real estate sales become increasingly more complicated. The "contract-to-close" period is among the most important in real estate. All the hard work of finding a buyer for your listing, working with the buyer's agent and negotiating the offer, and getting that offer ratified are just the beginning. Failure to attend to even one of a myriad of details during this period can threaten to undermine even the most solid-looking sale — which could jeopardize not only your commission but your relationship with your client as well (which could consequently put an end to a referral stream). For these reasons, as real estate agents, we must take these processes very seriously.

This book aims to help you anticipate and avert those mini-disasters that could derail your transaction. Whether you're a brand-new agent who doesn't want to reinvent the proverbial wheel or an experienced agent who simply wants to hone your own contract-to-settlement checklist, this book will help you continue guiding your clients to a successful settlement, collecting commission checks, and cultivating long-lasting personal and professional relationships with your clients.

What follows is my personal contract-to-close process, as it relates to duties of a buyer agent. I recommend that you read through what I do, and why, and then create your own checklist based on what you already do that works, and what you can take from my own system. As much as I love technology (and I really, really do!), I've kept my system rather low-tech. Real estate is, for the time being at least, a paper-based business. That is changing, of course, and the way we work will change. For now, though, I've found low-tech works best. There are many wonderful programs and systems out there for agents who are more technologically inclined. The system in this book can easily be tailored to an online platform. What's more important than the technology (whether you choose low- or high-tech) is the logic behind the system. Why do we do this action now? What are the situations we're trying to "pre-solve" or avert? The "why" is significantly more important than the "how."

This book provides a very basic, chronological framework for tracking the many details involved in the typical residential real estate transaction. Obviously, different jurisdictions will handle these details differently. Use good judgment in following these instructions (or not following them). Consult your broker or manager with questions about how to interpret the sales contract. Follow his or her advice, always.

Phase 1:
Once the contract is ratified

We'll start chronologically, from the time you get a listing under contract.

In the not-too-distant past, many agents — myself included — used "classification folders" to store the paperwork generated by a transaction. A classification folder is a pressboard folder divided into several different sections called "partitions." These folders come in legal and letter sizes. These classification folders were considered a real estate agent's best weapon to combat the huge amounts of paper that real estate transactions would produce. The average agent might simply carry around his or her transaction paperwork in a plain manila folder, and as a result finding a termite report or contract addendum on demand could become a comical exercise. Using some kind of paper-management system was (and still is) crucial especially if you're a new (or newish agent). Appearing organized is nearly as important as *being* organized!

Getting organized

It might have been common to label the six partitions of a listing folder as follows:

1. Miscellaneous (inside front cover): For your contract-to-close checklist and other items that may not fit into the other following tabs.

2. Sales Contract: This will be reserved for your working version of the sales contract (with older, unratified versions behind it).

3. Buyer-Agency Forms: This tab will house your buyer-agency agreement, along with any other disclosures (Affiliated

Business Arrangement statement, financial information statement, etc.) that you're responsible for executing.

4. Showings: This tab will house the MLS listings that you've shown your buyers.

5. Home Inspection: This tab will contain the home inspection report, along with paperwork associated with any subsequent negotiations.

6. Offers (inside back cover): Save any unratified offers in this tab.

These days, with the advent of electronic signing, transactions don't generate the same levels of extraneous paper as they used to. That said, real estate contracts are still complicated documents comprised of many different parts. As a result, you will want to create some kind of online, possibly cloud-based contract-management protocol to keep yourself and your transactions organized and orderly.

My "classification folder" model, above, is easily enough tailored to an online environment. Each transaction would get a new folder on your computer's hard drive or your cloud-based drive — and within each transaction folder, perhaps you create subfolders for things like the sales agreement, the home-inspection negotiation documentation, etc. No matter what, you'll want to save these documents with easily searchable file names so that you always know what's in a document just by its descriptive name (For instance, "1234 Main Street fully executed listing agreement.pdf")

You can use this manual as a kind of working transaction checklist, but you may well want to create your own checklist, tailored to your own system and market. If you're using a low-tech approach similar to mine, you will want to print your contract-to-close checklist. Once the classification folder is set up, place this on top of the "MISCELLANEOUS" tab at the front of the classification folder.

At this point, you know that you have a "meeting of the minds" between the buyer and seller, but you want to make sure that you have all the paperwork properly executed. So, you should go through the full contract, page by page, and make sure you have everything you need to prove that the contract is ratified (signatures by all parties where you need them, changes initialed by all parties). Your office also probably has some kind of in-office checklist of required documents. Collate the contract and check the required pages against your office's checklist. If you find that you're missing pages, initials, or signatures, it's much easier to circle back with the buyer agent at this point than it will become later. Additionally, many offices have policies that say you won't be paid in a timely fashion if some required documents aren't executed properly. Now is the time to deal with any missing initials or signatures.

Up to this point, the working contract will consist of possibly hundreds of pages, many duplicates, and will be in a very disorganized state. From that disorganized mess, we must pull out the required pages to create the final ratified contract. You will need to clear a space in order to work. First, retrieve a copy of the office checklist for ratified contracts. Then, begin looking for the individual elements to create the contract (the fully executed pages of the Sales Contract, with all initials and signatures in the appropriate places; any required addenda; etc.). Working form by form, ensure that you have everything on the office checklist. If something is missing (pages or initials), you'll need to follow up with the other agent. It's possible that that initial or page is still in your email as an attachment. If you determine after a full search that there are pages or initials that are missing, it may be necessary to reach out to the other agent to get them or to have the client or customer execute them subsequently. Once the file is complete, make one copy of the document and set that aside. Two-hole punch the original version of the document and place it in classification folder at the "SALES CONTRACT" tab.

You will need to save the document as an electronic file. PDF is the most common file format for these kinds of electronic files. There are several ways to do this (scan it, fax it to an electronic fax number, etc.). Once you've saved the executed contract on your hard drive, you'll want to email a copy of it to the seller, along with the text from the "what to expect" letter (see fig.). The subject line should read something like: "What to expect now that you're under contract." Paste the text of the letter into the body of the email, and send.

Keeping track of contact information

Whether you keep all your contacts in an electronic or paper format, make sure you have the contact information of all the participants in the transaction:

- The settlement company (usually named in the contract, though you may need to do an internet search for full contact information)
- The purchaser (you can usually find this on the buyer's earnest money deposit check)
- The buyer's agent (this may be in the contract, or you may need to look up the buyer agent's contact information online or in your MLS database)
- The loan officer (from the preapproval letter)

For each person, open a new, blank contact in your contact software and input the necessary contact information.

Keeping track of upcoming deadlines

Keeping track of contingency-expiration deadlines becomes one of a listing agents' primary jobs during the contract-to-close period. You'll want to note all of these deadlines in your datebook or electronic calendar. From the contract, make a note of all the relevant contingency-expiration and settlement dates. The settlement date will be a date certain that is written into the contract. The contingency expirations will often need to be calculated from the date of ratification.

- Home inspection contingency expiration

- Financing contingency expiration
- Appraisal contingency expiration

Do the same for the settlement date. For the settlement date, I like to add it to the calendar at 1:00 pm on the date of settlement given in the contract and add "TENTATIVE" — so I don't inadvertently schedule something at the same time. (I like to schedule settlements for either 1:00 pm or 2:00 pm, as I find this gives everyone time to do things they need to do on the settlement date — the buyer may need to go to the bank to get a cashier's check or arrange a wire transfer, the buyer agent may need to meet the buyers at the property for a pre-settlement walk-through inspection; the buyer may want to eat lunch before settlement. After the settlement, the seller may need to get to the bank to deposit a proceeds check, and the buyer may want to return to the property to check security or to change the locks. A mid-day settlement is not always feasible for a variety of reasons, but when possible it allows for all of these tasks to be completed, both before and after settlement.)

Following office procedures

Your office likely has some protocol for accounting for the new sale and for handling the earnest money deposit (if your broker will hold the earnest-money deposit). At this point, follow whatever that protocol is. Most offices have some kind of in-take form you'll fill out, either on paper or electronically. Once this in-take form is completed, print two copies of it. One of these copies will be two-hole punched and will be placed in the classification case folder on top of the Sales Contract.

The other copy will be turned into the office admin with a copy of the contract and the earnest-money deposit within 24 hours of ratification. Consult your office checklist if you're unsure what needs to be turned in. Ensure that you have a copy of the earnest-money deposit in the green classification file with the contract.

Most jurisdictions have a time frame within which earnest-money deposits must be processed. For our seller's sake, we want to make sure that this time frame is met. It is sometimes necessary to contact the buyer agent to make sure that certain tasks are addressed in a timely fashion. This is one of those items. Even though it may not be your duty to deposit this check, you still need to verify that it has been done. If you deem it necessary to check, you'll need to contact the buyer agent, by phone or email, and say something along the lines of, "I'm just checking in to make sure that the earnest-money was turned in to your accounting department. Can you please confirm?" If the answer is anything but a resounding "yes" (and some buyer agents will be annoyed at this question), you'll want to do some more sleuthing. There are significant ramifications to your seller if the earnest money is not handled properly. Any buyer agent who becomes annoyed at your asking such a necessary question bears a close watch during the transaction.

Delivering copies of the ratified contract

If your contract has been ratified by electronic signatures, your client likely already has a copy of the final contract. If not, make sure to email a copy to him or her. Additionally, the buyer's loan officer will need a copy, as well as the title company.

Scheduling the home inspection

Usually, within a few days of ratification, the buyer may wish to have a home inspection performed — this will usually have been negotiated in the contract. You'll work with the listing agent to coordinate the scheduling of the home inspection with the seller. It is generally the buyer agent's responsibility to schedule the home inspection in accordance with the terms of the Sales Contract. Once you find out when the buyer wishes to perform the home inspection, follow up with the listing to confirm that this time will work. If it won't, you will need to coordinate with the buyer and listing agent to find a time that's mutually acceptable to the buyer and seller. When the home inspection is set, set the inspection up as an appointment in your calendar.

Every contract is different. No matter what, you'll want to prepare your buyer for the home inspection process BEFORE it happens. Review the pertinent details of the contract that relate to property condition. Are there property-condition items that the seller will be obligated to address after the inspection that are not subject to a negotiation? Are there items that would need to be negotiated, or a credit given after the inspection? It has been my experience that buyers are generally much more reasonable and inclined to rational negotiation if I've fully prepared them for what the home inspection negotiation looks and feels like. These conversations are much easier to navigate before the fact than after.

Coordinating the buyer's loan application

Most real estate sales contracts call for the buyer to submit a formal loan application within a certain number of days after contract ratification. You'll want to ensure that the buyer has done this. It is the buyer agent's responsibility to ensure that this happens in a timely fashion.

Following up on the delivery of any association documents

If the listing is in a condominium association, homeowner's association, or cooperative association, you will probably need to follow up with the listing agent to coordinate the delivery of association resale documents to the buyer.

Scheduling settlement

It many jurisdictions, it is the norm for the buyer's agent to send the settlement company a copy of the contract and schedule settlement. Here is some sample text you may wish to use: "I have just ratified a contract (attached) for one of our clients, and your company has been selected as the settlement agent. The contract calls for settlement on _____ (date). If possible, we would prefer a mid-day settlement that day; 1:00 pm or 2:00 pm would be ideal. Would you please check your calendar and let me know if you can accommodate one of those time slots? I will be in touch shortly to confirm your receipt of this contract." Contact the settlement processor by phone to ensure receipts of the contract.

Phase 2:
After the home inspection

After the home inspection, the buyer will likely execute some sort of document (I'll call it the "home inspection notice" that will either 1) initiate a negotiation of items that the buyer would like repaired or for which the buyer would like a credit or price reduction, or 2) void the contract. The home inspection notice will also probably be accompanied by a copy of the inspection report if the buyer has decided to enter into a negotiation with the seller. The date by which you should deliver these documents to the listing agent and seller has probably been specified in the contract. By the close of business on the date specified in the contract, ensure that you have delivered these documents, as appropriate.

Negotiating the home inspection

When you have sent the home inspection notice and report to the listing agent, you may wish to reach out to the listing agent to confirm delivery of the documents and to contextualize any requests the buyer is making. This is your opportunity to sell the value in your buyer's position.

It is likely that the sellers may wish to make a counter proposal to the buyer's request. They will have a certain number of days to respond. If they do, they will memorialize those changes on the home inspection notice and send that notice back through the listing agent. This process may go back and forth a few times.

Different contracts handle these negotiations differently — some provide for the negotiation to be completed within a certain time period; others allow for the negotiation to continue as long as it takes to come to a meeting of the minds.

Eventually, all parties will come to terms. At that point, print or scan the home inspection notice, and either two-hole punch it for insertion into the classification folder in the home inspection partition, along with the complete home inspection report; or save it to your electronic folder on your computer.

If the contract is to be released as a result of the home inspection (or for any other reason, for that matter), ensure that the release, fully executed and signed by all necessary parties, is turned in to the office manager or admin.

Phase 3:
Within a week of ratification

Send the seller information on changing their address with the Postal Service. The subject line might read: "Have you changed your address yet?" Here's some sample verbiage:

> Dear Buyer,
>
> As we get closer to settlement, I wanted to pass along a link for changing your address with the Postal Service, in case you haven't already done this:
>
> https://moversguide.usps.com
>
> As always, if there's anything I can do to assist you as we get closer to settlement, please don't hesitate to call or email!
>
> Warm regards,
>
> Kevin
>
> P.S. As a reminder, if you haven't done so already, you may want to go ahead notify your utility providers (phone, gas, electric, cable, or water) that you'll be moving in a few weeks. You'll need to have the utilities in your name through the day of settlement. Please let me know if I can help you with any of this!

Following up on the delivery of association documents

If you haven't heard from the listing agent regarding the delivery of the association documents, you may wish to check in now.

Providing buyer's contact information to settlement company

Every settlement company requires certain information from the buyer as they prepare for settlement (Social Security number, new address, etc.). Usually, the settlement company will email a questionnaire with information to fill out on the buyer's behalf, or to forward on to the buyer. If you have not received such a questionnaire, contact the settlement processor by phone or email two ask if he or she has a similar questionnaire for your buyer. Once the questionnaire arrives, forward the document to the buyer. Within a few days, follow up with the buyer to make sure he or she has filled out the document and returned it to the settlement processor.

Verifying if the transaction qualifies for reissue rate on the title insurance

Check to see if the transaction qualifies for reissue title insurance rate. The cost of a new title insurance policy is charged to the buyer at settlement. This is one of the most expensive items charged to the buyer for the transaction. If the property has transferred in recent years to the current seller, the transaction may qualify for a discounted title insurance rate ("reissue rate") for the buyer. Check the public record to see how long the current seller has owned the property. If the current seller has owned the property for less than five years, say, contact the listing agent to determine if the seller has the copy of the title insurance policy. If the current owner does not have a copy of his or her title insurance policy, contact the settlement company for advice.

Following up regarding keys and garage-door openers

Some of the properties that you sell likely have garages with automatic garage door openers (or, "clickers"). The new buyer may wish to use the garage when he or she moves. Because of this, you want to make sure that the sellers do not inadvertently pack the garage-door clickers during their more. First, check the MLS printout to see if garage parking is included in the sale. If it is, contact the listing agent to inquire about the whereabouts of the clickers and extra sets of keys. Ask the listing agent to bring the clickers to settlement, or to leave them in the property (some agents like to leave them in the refrigerator, where they're less likely to be scooped up inadvertently by movers) for upi to retrieve during the pre-settlement walk-through inspection.

Phase 4:
Two weeks before settlement

Scheduling the termite inspection

Many times, the sales contract is contingent on a termite inspection; and many loan programs require one. Typically, it will fall to the buyer agent to coordinate the termite inspection. Consult the sales contract, to see whose responsibility it is. If it is the buyer agent's responsibility, coordinate with the listing agent. Typically, the buyer client does not need to attend the termite inspection. Once the termite inspection is scheduled, create an appointment on your calendar.

Ensuring the delivery of the appraisal

You will want to make sure that the appraisal has been received by the loan officer in a timely fashion. Contact the loan officer by phone or email to inquire as to the status of the appraisal. If the appraisal has not been received yet, ask the loan officer when he or she believes the appraisal will be available. If the appraisal has been received by the loan officer, ask the loan officer to forward a copy of the appraisal to the buyer. If the value has come in below the sales price, you will want to consult the contract for next steps. It's possible that the buyer will formally ask the seller to lower the sales price to the appraised value. You'll want to follow up with the buyer to establish the buyer's intent. If the appraisal comes back at value or higher, you will need to consult the sales contract to find out the protocol for formally removing the appraisal contingency.

Determining the need for a Power of Attorney

Occasionally, you'll encounter a situation where your buyer will be unavailable to attend settlement. In such cases, it may be necessary for the buyer to have a power of attorney who can sign the closing documents for him or her (if allowed by the buyer's loan). Contact the buyer to ask if he or she intends to attend settlement. If it turns out that the buyer will be unable to attend settlement, put the buyer in touch with the loan officer and settlement agent who can coordinate drafting the necessary documents. Follow up with both the buyer and the settlement processor to ensure everything is carried out properly.

Phase 5:
One week before settlement

Confirming the MLS status

Depending on your MLS's rules, you may wish to confirm the change of the status of the listing from active to "CONTINGENT" to "UNDER CONTRACT," if all contingencies have been satisfied. If they haven't, you'll want to follow up with the listing agent until they are.

Confirming the completion of all inspections

Ensure that all inspections have been completed. At this point, you want to make sure that all inspections (termite inspection, home inspection, radon inspection, etc.) have been completed and all necessary documentation is in the file. First, check the sales contract to see which inspections, if any, are required. If the termite inspection has been performed, is the termite report in the file? If the termite report indicates either an active infestation of termites or structural and as a result of an infestation, it may be necessary for the seller to remediate. If this is the case, you'll need to be in touch with the listing agent to coordinate such work. Once the work has been done, it may be necessary to have a subsequent termite inspection to prove that the home is now free of termites or termite damage. Once the termite inspection is clear, email a copy of the report to the settlement processor, and file a copy in the classification folder.

Finalizing preparations for settlement day

The day of settlement can be a busy and stressful day for your buyer clients. You'll want to do everything you can to minimize any stress they are under, including providing them as much information as possible about the schedule of events for the day.

Here's an email you may wish to send with the possible subject of "Settlement day is fast approaching!"

Dear Buyer,

Settlement is next week! Can you believe it's almost here?

The day of settlement can be a busy and stressful day, so I want to do whatever I can to minimize any stress you'll be under that day. My first suggestion is that, if it's at all possible, you should take the day off from work on settlement day. I find that my clients are much happier if they can take the day off from work that day.

The settlement is scheduled to take place at _____ ____ _____ (settlement company name / "our office") at _____ (street address) at _____ a.m./p.m.; the phone number is _____, just in case you need it. The nearest Metro station is ____ _____.
Please let us know if you need driving directions. Parking is _____ (whatever you can find out from the settlement processor).

The sellers will have vacated the property prior to this so that we can conduct our pre-settlement walk-through inspection. I'll follow up with you in coming days to coordinate scheduling the walk-through.

As always, if there's anything I can do to assist you over the next week, please don't hesitate to ask.

Warm regards,

Kevin

P.S. As a reminder, if you haven't done so already, you may want to go ahead and have the utilities (phone, gas, electric, cable — the settlement company will handle the water service) transferred into your name as of the day AFTER settlement. Please let me know if you need any assistance!

Scan the text for any information that may need to be tailored to the transaction (settlement company, location of settlement, nearest metro, parking information, time of walk-through), amend the note, and send the message to the buyer.

Confirming the completion of repairs

Often, as a result of the home inspection, the seller will have agreed to perform certain repairs to the property prior to settlement. You'll want to check the status of those repairs. Contact the listing agent and ask if all the repairs have been completed and if they have not, find out what is outstanding. Also, ask if the listing agent would send you copies of the receipts for the work that has been done prior to settlement. Once that documentation has been emailed to you, forward it to the buyer prior to the walk-through.

Scheduling the walk-through inspection

Reach out to the buyer and the listing agent to schedule the pre-settlement walk-through inspection. Generally speaking, the walk-through inspection should be conducted after the sellers have vacated the property but before settlement. If the wishes to conduct the walk-through at another time (say, the day before settlement), you'll want to coordinate with the buyer and listing agent.

Ordering the home warranty

A home warranty is a service contract from an outside vendor that covers the repair or replacement of many of the most frequently occurring breakdowns of home system components and appliances.

Check the sales contract to determine if a home warranty has been specified. If a home warranty has been specified, and it is to be paid for by the seller at settlement, you'll need to make sure that you have the home-warranty order forms in the file, prior to settlement.

Obtaining the overage check, if applicable

In transactions where our buyers have written a large earnest money deposit check, we may need to obtain what is called an "overage check" from your broker's accounting department (if your broker is the escrow agent). You need an overage anytime you are representing buyers who have written an earnest money deposit check that is larger than the gross commission owed to your broker on the transaction. If the earnest money deposit check is larger than gross commission, check with your broker or office admin request.

Confirming how buyer will hold title

Email information to the purchasers (if they are a couple, married or not) about how they will hold title. One of the questions that the purchasers will be asked at settlement — if they are a couple — is how they intend to take title to the new property. It's a complicated question and they will want to have thought about this prior to settlement. If the purchasers have questions about this, put them in touch with the settlement processor or attorney for assistance.

Phase 6:
A few days before settlement

Ensuring buyer has arranged to obtain funds to the settlement company for closing

Ensure that purchaser has obtained or wired closing funds for settlement. If necessary, put buyer in touch with settlement processor for wiring instructions.

Obtaining a copy of the settlement statement

Coordinate getting a copy of the preliminary settlement statement from the settlement company. The settlement statement is a form used by the settlement agent (also called the closing agent) to itemize all charges imposed upon a borrower and seller for a real estate transaction. It gives each party a complete list of their incoming and outgoing funds. The statutes of the Real Estate Settlement Procedures Act (RESPA) require the form be used as the standard real estate settlement form in all transactions in the United States that involve federally related mortgage loans. RESPA states that a buyer should be given a copy of the settlement statement least three days prior to settlement.

 Most buyers and sellers study the statement on their own, with their real estate agent, and with the settlement agent. The more people who review it, the more likely that errors will be detected and corrected as soon as possible to avoid a delay in settlement. Therefore, we want to make sure you and the loan officer review the preliminary settlement statement BEFORE the buyer receives it. If you have not received the preliminary statement by now, contact the settlement processor to ask for the most up-to-date version; also ask if the loan officer has reviewed it yet.

Sending a copy of the settlement statement to the buyer

Send the HUD-1 to the purchaser. Open a new email message with a subject line of "Preliminary settlement statement attached." Attach the up-to-date PDF version of the settlement statement.

> Dear Buyer ---
>
> Attached, please find the settlement statement that you'll sign at the settlement table. The settlement statement is a form used by the settlement attorney to itemize all the charges imposed on a borrower and seller for a real estate transaction. It's a snap-shot of all the money involved in the transaction. It gives each party a complete list of their incoming and outgoing funds.
>
> The settlement statement is required on all real estate transactions in the United States that involve federally related mortgage loans, like yours. By law, you're supposed to receive a preliminary version of this document at least three days prior to settlement.
>
> I have reviewed the document, as has your loan officer. It may look a little daunting, but the settlement attorney will review this with you, line-by-line, at the settlement table, so you'll know exactly what everything means. But feel free to take a look now and let us know if you have any questions.
>
> As always, if there's anything I can do to assist you in coming days, please don't hesitate to ask.
>
> Warm regards,
>
> Kevin

P.S.: Don't forget to bring your ID to settlement!

P.P.S.: As a reminder, if you haven't done so already, you may want to go ahead and have the utilities (phone, gas, electric, cable --- the settlement company will handle the water service) transferred into your name as of the day AFTER settlement.

Phase 7:
The day of settlement

Conducting the final walk-through inspection

A final walk-through is an inspection performed anywhere from a few hours to a few days before settlement. Its primary purpose is to make certain that the property is in the condition you agreed to buy — that agreed-upon repairs, if any, were made — and nothing has gone wrong with the home since the buyer last looked at it. Many jurisdictions have forms that are to be completed during or after the walk-through. Review local requirements with your broker.

Conveying the walk-through results with the listing agent

Contact the listing agent about the results of the walk-through inspection. If there are items that remain unresolved, the listing agent may want to contact the seller for a status on these items. It's possible that some items may need to be dealt with at the settlement table. If this is the case, you may want to contact the settlement agent or attorney to apprise him or her of that situation.

Made in the USA
Thornton, CO
04/26/23 21:12:01

708cb12b-d9dd-4bab-ac59-ec397bfb5dbaR01